302.23

This book is to be returned on or before date stamped below. 302

TO3946   302·23

media watch

newspapers

Lucy Williams

Wayland

media watch

Advertising
Newspapers
Magazines
TV and Video

Series Editor: James Kerr
Designer: John Christopher

Consultant: Julian Bowker,
Education Officer, British Film Institute.

Front cover picture: *USA Today*

First published in 1993 by
Wayland (Publishers) Ltd
61 Western Road, Hove
East Sussex, BN3 1JD

British Library Cataloguing in Publication Data
Williams, Lucy
Newspapers. - (Media Watch Series)
I. Title II. Series
302.23

ISBN 0-7502-0728-0

Typeset by Strong Silent Type
Printed and bound in Spain by Graficas Estella.

Picture Acknowledgements
The publisher would like to thank the following for providing the pictures used in this book: Ancient Art & Architecture Collection 19; DLP 22-3; Eye Ubiquitous (Paul Seheult) 33,34,43, (Ian Yates) 24; Format (Melanie Friend) 28, (Jenny Matthews) 32, (Joanna O'Brien) 27; John Frost Newspapers 4,20 (bottom),21; Impact (Alan Brooke) 42, (Piers Cavendish) 16, (Brian Harris) 39; Network (Barry Lewis) 18, (John Sturrock) 40; Popperfoto 7,14-15,41; Topham 5, 6, 9, 12, 13, 20, (top), 25, 29, 30, 36; Wayland Picture Library 8,10-11,17.
The artwork is by John Christopher.

contents

The history of newspapers 4

Hot metal to computers: how papers are printed 10

Scoop! 18

The editorial team 24

More than the news 32

The freedom of the press 38

Glossary 45

Further reading 47

Further information & notes for teachers 47

Index 48

The history of
newspapers

The first papers containing news were handwritten by the Chinese from AD 618. Long before the printing press was invented in Europe, the Chinese were also using metal type, ink and paper to print.

In Europe, news was carried by word of mouth, often by travelling people and professional bards who would sing their 'news songs' for money. The first European books were printed in the 1450s, but few people could read so there was no public demand for newspapers. It was not until the 1600s that the first newspaper was published, in Germany.

The rise of the European newspaper industry began in Holland. By 1626 the Dutch were publishing over 100 news-sheets. These publications did not cover a selection of events, like modern newspapers. Instead, each issue contained a sensational description of a single incident, such as an earthquake, which had often happened months or years before.

Early newspapers looked like books, and were passed around among readers for months or even years. Up to 1,000 copies of each 8-12 page edition were produced, in small print set in single columns. There were few headlines to break up the dense design, so that as much news could be crammed

BELOW Customers in coffee houses shared newspapers

in as possible. Newspapers were usually printed in cities, and some journals offered a blank last page, where readers could write in their own news before sending the publication to their friends in the country.

Newspapers were expensive, so sellers often hired them out by the hour, and only sent them on to subscribers at the end of the day, when they had been read many times. Pubs and coffee houses also catered for the growing interest in current affairs by renting out newspapers. For those who could not read there was usually a 'read aloud' service.

Gradually newspapers were published regularly, such as the English *diurnalls* (weeklies) of the 1640s. Different types of newspapers sprang up: the *Intelli-gencer* reported the government's point of view; the *Coranto* covered foreign affairs; the *Mercury* contained the opinions of many different people on all sorts of subjects. In Venice, newspapers were known as gazettes, as they were sold for the price of one gazetta – a coin.

Newspapers began to cover more recent news, and were published as events happened. For instance, the English Civil War, which began in 1642, led to thousands of publications being set up. In 1650 the world's first daily newspaper started in Leipzig, Germany. Across Europe, the market for newspapers grew steadily among the general public, and weekly papers were set up along trade routes. By 1750, in London

ABOVE
An early advertisement for a newspaper that is still published today.

5

alone there were five daily newspapers. With industrial progress in the nineteenth century, the mass production of paper became possible, making paper more available and less expensive. New schooling laws meant that more people could read, and growing cities provided not only an audience for newspapers but also a base and a source of news.

The newspaper industry became part of the economy. New printing and paper-production methods used for newspapers began to be used in the packaging of other products, such as foodstuffs. Advertising carried in newspapers encouraged people to buy all sorts of goods. News itself was boosted by new technology. In Britain, the electric telegraph was used for the first time in 1845 to send information to papers outside London. In the 1870s the first train services for distributing newspapers were introduced.

The latest news became something which could be bought and sold when news agencies were set up. These organizations collected news reports and then sold stories to newspapers. In 1851, Paul Julius Reuter set up the London office of Reuters, now one of the biggest news agencies in the world, with the aim of providing an international news service.

**BELOW
A wood engraving from a newspaper of 1820 shows a police raid and gunfight**.

**RIGHT
'Wire' operators in the 1950s send news worldwide on Reuters' radio teletype machines**.

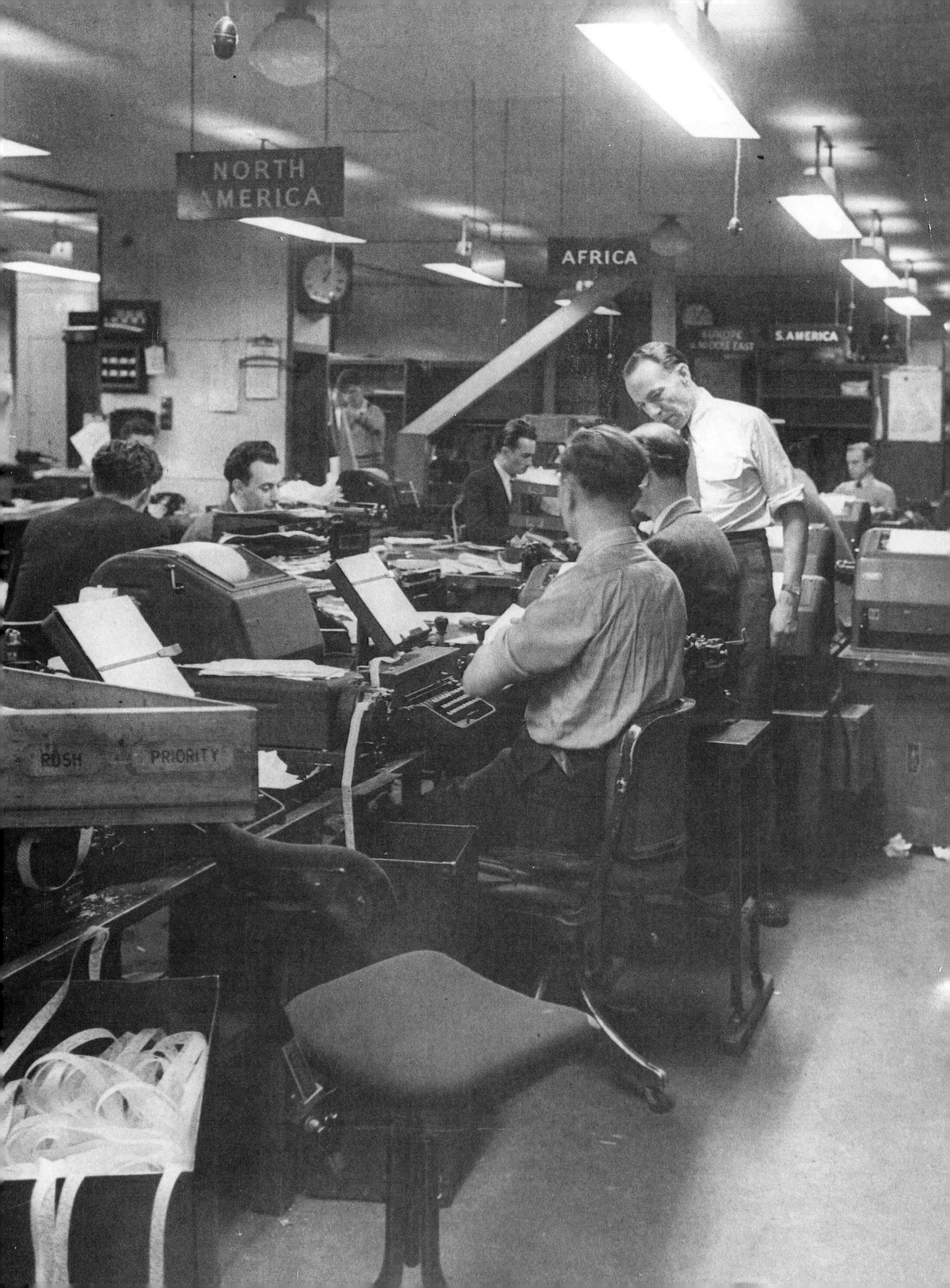
NORTH AMERICA
AFRICA
S. AMERICA
RUSH
PRIORITY

The British papers that were based outside London and other major cities set up the Press Association in 1868 to provide local papers with a collective source of national news. In America, A.N. Kellogg sent editors half-made newspapers on to which they printed their own news.

Today the quest for speed means that news is beamed across the world via satellite almost as it happens. Journalists covering the 1991 Gulf War carried portable satellite phones to get their copy back fast from the war zone; a far cry from the carrier pigeons used in the First World War.

By the beginning of the twentieth century, newspapers had become big business. Early newspapers were usually owned by the printers, who were powerful because they controlled the presses. Over the years, ownership passed from the printers to booksellers, then to wealthy landowners and finally to businessmen. Family firms developed into large companies headed by powerful directors who became known as 'press barons'. In Britain, Lords Rothermere, Northcliffe and Beaverbrook controlled large sections of the press, while in America, William Randolph Hearst dominated.

Today, newspaper owners often control multinational companies which own smaller companies in various industries throughout the world. One of the most powerful of these newspaper tycoons is Rupert Murdoch, who owns some of the world's most successful newspapers, as well as television stations and film companies.

BELOW
Satellite dishes beam news around the world.

**ABOVE Australian businessman
Rupert Murdoch has made a fortune
in the modern newspaper industry.**

Modern newspapers can be categorized according to how often and when they are published, and which section of society their content is aimed at. National newspapers are based in cities and are distributed around the whole country, often carrying international news. Local papers cover a specific area. They feature stories that will interest a local readership, and have smaller circulations than the nationals.

Many cities have their own daily paper, which can be a morning or an evening paper. These papers can have several editions for distribution purposes; for instance, the County edition goes out to the countryside while the City Night Final is sold in the city centre.

Some daily regional papers publish national news stories alongside local news. This is rarely the case with weekly regional papers, the majority of which concentrate exclusively on local matters.

Early newspapers were hand-made books painstakingly printed on high-quality paper. By contrast, modern newspapers are mass-produced in two main sizes and styles; broadsheets are 42 by 60 cm, while tabloids are smaller, around 28 by 40 cm. They are cheap compared to papers produced in earlier times and have a short lifespan.

Activities
• Go to your local library or the office of your local newspaper and in the files look up local or national newspapers from the same day and month 25, 50 and 100 years ago.

• From one or more of the papers you have found, choose the stories that you find most interesting and rewrite them into a 200-word 'Peeps from the Past' column to be used in a modern paper.

• Note how the style of writing and page design has changed over the years. Now take a story from today's newspaper and write it in the style used 100 years ago.

Hot metal to computers:
how papers are printed

The newspaper industry as we know it today has developed alongside the technology available to print papers. As this technology became faster and more efficient, so newspapers were published more regularly and covered more recent news.

The first printing press, invented around 1450, was operated by hand. Each page of type, called a forme, was laid on a movable flat bed. The type was then inked with a leather and horsehair printer's ball dipped in a mixture of oil and lamp-black, a colouring substance made from soot. The platen, a large wooden or metal plate, was then pressed down on to the forme so that a printed impression was left on a sheet of paper inserted in between the two parts.

As demand for newspapers increased, it became clear that old printing methods were not fast enough. A new source of power was needed to work

BELOW From left to right: compositors choose type which is made up into sentences, then inked with a roller ready to be put under the press (far right). In the background a man is hanging printed papers up to dry.

the heavy print machinery. This was found when steam began to be used as a power source for engineering at the beginning of the nineteenth century.

The steam press still worked on the flatbed 'letterpress' principle of the early presses, but could produce more than 1,000 sheets per hour from a massive, heavy, cast-iron frame. A lot of energy was needed, as for each imprint the page of type had to be raised and lowered.

The invention of the rotary press in 1846 meant that papers could be printed faster, as type cast in metal was locked on to a cylinder and rolled on to the paper. However, using single sheets of paper, which were mainly made from rags, slowed the printing process down. In 1865, in America, a Philadelphia newspaper became the first to use a roll of paper, called a web, to feed its rotary press continuously. This meant around 10,000 eight-page papers could be printed in one hour.

LEFT
In the days of hot metal, printers check a newly cast cylindrical mould.

In the 1880s it was discovered that wood pulp could be used to make paper, thereby reducing the cost of newsprint. In 1889 the rotary press was improved so that it printed the paper on both sides and then cut and folded the sheets.

In the 1960s, a major development revolutionized the printing process. The web-offset method uses printing plates that, instead of being cast in metal, are produced by exposure to a film negative. Instead of a heavy type forme, a lightweight photographic plate is produced. In the web-offset printing process the paper does not touch the printing plate. Instead, the inked image on the plate is 'offset' on to a rubber roller, which is then rolled on to the web of paper to print.

BELOW
A modern printing works, with webs of paper.

Today, newspapers use both the letterpress and web-offset methods, although web-offset produces a higher-quality image and is more often used for colour printing. Putting the letters together on the page – the process called composing – has also undergone a transformation. The first compositors, or typesetters, were known as the aristocrats of the printing world. They used trays of metal letters from which they selected individual letters at great speed. The letters were fitted into place to create a mirror image of the page in the forme. Thus the compositors had to be skilled at reading backwards. In the 1860s, the invention of the Hattersley composing machine meant that the compositor used a keyboard to select the letters. The Linotype machine, invented in America in the 1880s, used hot molten metal to cast new type letters from moulds each time they were needed to make a line of type.

In the days of hot-metal production, stories were typed onto small sheets of copy paper by journalists using manual typewriters. The copy was then altered on paper by sub-editors. The stories were then passed to the compositors, who transferred them from paper to metal. Advances in computer technology since the 1960s have meant that stories can be typeset on screen and printed directly on to photographic paper, ending the need for metal type and typesetters.

LEFT
The former *Daily Sketch* newsroom – not a computer in sight!

ABOVE
A journalist
at work
on a visual
display unit
at The
Independent.

piece of paper printed with a grid of the same size as the newspaper's page. Once the page is made up it is checked by a journalist known as a 'stone sub-editor'. It is then photographed by a large camera to create the page-sized negative used for printing.

Photographs used to illustrate news stories are made ready for printing by being photographed through a fine screen, which transforms them into a pattern of different-sized dots. These patterns are transferred to the printing plate. Although all of the dots are solid black, they are of different sizes, and give an

**RIGHT
Pasting
up a page
on to a
galley
sheet
attached
to the
'stone'.**

Today, computers with laser printers are capable of producing every kind of typeface, and news-production software has been created. Reporters type their copy on to a computer visual display unit (VDU), and send it electronically to the sub-editors, who typeset the stories on screen. The stories are then printed out on a laser printer and 'pasted up'.

In the paste-up department of a newspaper, production staff make up the pages by following a page plan designed by a sub-editor. Typeset stories are cut out using a metal ruler and scalpel and are stuck down with hot wax on to a galley sheet. This is a large

illusion of different shades of grey when viewed from a short distance. These shades could not otherwise be achieved by a printing press, which can only produce solid colour. Lasers and computers are now being used to reproduce pictures.

Japan is at the forefront of continuing advances in newspaper technology. One development is video cameras, which allow pictures to be scanned into pages that have been designed on screen. There are also plans to produce fax newspapers which will be printed out on machines in people's homes.

Activities

• Find as many different ways of reproducing the written word as you can. You might include methods like potato printing, typewriting, transfer lettering, handwriting, printing block set, stencil, photocopier, visual display unit.

• Try out the different media for printing individual words or whole sentences and compare the time taken and the finished product. Under what circumstances would you use each of the different methods?

Scoop!

Every morning, most newspaper offices receive bundles of letters and press releases about events which the public feels should be publicized in the paper. During the day, reporters take lots of telephone calls informing them of all kinds of events, from major accidents and scandals to local fêtes and minor disputes.

Journalists scour other media, including television, radio and rival newspapers, to find story leads. Reporters also cover the meetings and decisions of national and local governments, magistrates' courts and crown courts, and thousands of other organizations, from residents' associations to trade unions. From this vast flow of information, journalists have to decide what to include in the paper. Their decision is based on the concept of news value.

To have news value, a story must be fresh, relevant and remarkable. A fresh story will have just happened, or if it has not just happened it must be unknown to the general public. If the news is part of a long-running story, a new development must have taken place. The story must also be relevant to its readers. It should affect their lives directly, or interest them by being written in a way that they can understand and relate to.

Lastly, but most importantly, the story must be remarkable. An event such as street lamps being lit may be recent

BELOW
A photographer wires pictures home from abroad.

and relevant to readers, but it happens every night and will not excite their interest. Decisions concerning news value are subjective – they depend on the person making them. What is considered worth printing as news has changed as the newspaper industry has developed.

When there were no other mass methods of communication, newspapers were free to report events without having to stick closely to the facts. Their accounts of sea monsters, witches and ghosts often seem nearer to fiction than news to today's reader.

As printing technology developed and became ever faster, so did methods of communication. Papers were published more regularly and so could cover fresher news. However, the modern idea of news was still not fully developed. Today, the front page is used to carry the most important news of the day and to tempt readers to buy the paper. But until the 1870s, most papers were delivered by hand, and the front page, which carried advertising, was used as a wrapper to protect the contents.

ABOVE
The first issue of The *Daily Universal Register* from 1785, which became *The Times*.

Entire political speeches were reported, without any editing, in pages of dense type broken only by the name of the speaker. Long, unsigned commentary and opinion articles were also common.

In the 1870s, some American editors realized that more sensational stories and an eye-catching layout would sell more newspapers. In the 'New Journalism', which quickly spread across the Atlantic, both style and content changed.

ABOVE Advertising covers the front page of a 1906 edition of The *Daily Mail*.

The emphasis shifted to human interest stories: executions, divorces and murder hunts such as the search for Jack the Ripper in London in the late nineteenth century.

Newspapers aimed to entertain as well as to inform; reporters wrote dramatic descriptions of crimes and hangings, and sports reports, interviews and serialized novels were also introduced. Reporters were sent on sensational 'stunt' stories, dreamed up by editors to excite the readers. The *New York Herald* sponsored H.M. Stanley to travel to Africa to search for the lost explorer Dr David Livingstone. Newspapers championed favourite causes: Joseph Pulitzer of the New York-based *World* raised the money from his readers to build the base for the Statue of Liberty.

New design rules helped to make newspapers more reader-friendly. Big, bold banner headlines going right across the front page, more drawings and engravings, shorter paragraphs and cross heads – short headings within the text – made up a new tabloid style. Today, although most newspapers have the same news flowing into their newsrooms, editors treat it in different ways.

The tabloid press generally aim for a simple style that will be understood by all readers. Paragraphs and stories are kept short and headlines are big and bold. Stories and headlines are written to have an emotional impact; the aim is to make the reader laugh or cry. Humour, including puns and alliteration in headlines, is used to make the paper more entertaining.

The 'middle-market' press use the tabloid format, but present stories in a less sensational way. The broadsheet or 'quality' press make it their priority to inform. Stories are longer and more in-depth, and usually aim to deal less with personal details and more with facts. More complex vocabulary and less slang is used.

FAR LEFT
The historic event that took place on November 22 1963 is splashed across the front page of The *Dallas Morning News* using bold banner headlines and cross heads.

As well as treating the same news differently, tabloids and broadsheets consider different topics to be news. Tabloids include fewer 'serious' news items – such as politics and business stories – than broadsheets. Their reporting, of political stories in particular, tends to be biased. Tabloids cover even the minor antics of personalities such as royalty and pop, film and television stars. Broadsheets include more

ABOVE
Tabloids aim to sell newspapers by using amazing headlines.

international and political news, and, even if they take a particular point of view, usually allow more space for debate. The middle-market papers cover the ground between the tabloids and broadsheets.

As well as covering events as they happen, newspapers create news by investigative journalism. A reporter may receive a tip-off about a newsworthy event, which could range from political corruption to a star's love affair.

To research such stories, teams of reporters often go undercover. They sometimes work with an insider or 'off-the-record source', who will provide them with secret information but will not be named in the story. Investigative journalism can provide the most sensational but also the most dangerous stories. The stories can be dangerous for the paper to carry, for example the false report that appeared in a British tabloid claiming that Conservative politician Jeffery Archer had tried to bribe a prostitute. Working with the prostitute, the paper had gone to great lengths to try to prove the story by taping a meeting. But Mr Archer took the paper to court, where the paper was found guilty of libel and ordered to pay Mr Archer a large sum of money. Investigative journalism can carry other dangers; a journalist who goes under-cover to follow a tip-off about organized crime – for example a Mafia boss or a terrorist gang – could be risking his or her life.

**LEFT
Reporters often wait outside a subject's house for the chance of an interview.**

Activities
• Using a national tabloid and a broadsheet newspaper, find a story in each which covers the same event.
• Make a list of the differences in the way in which the story is written and laid out in each paper, including differences in vocabulary, grammar, use of slang and length.
• Now write your own story and headline on the subject of your choice, using the same facts, in both tabloid and broadsheet style.

The editorial team

Today's newspapers are competing with the electronic media – radio and television – to get the news to the public as quickly as possible. Speed and accuracy are the main aims in newspaper production. Deadlines – strict time limits on each stage of the process – ensure that production does not fall behind schedule. If papers are printed late, what were exclusive stories will have become common knowledge.

To put together quickly the many different elements that make up a newspaper requires teamwork. All the staff on a newspaper, from the journalists to the printers, are responsible for a different part of the process.

The editorial team, which includes journalists and photographers, aims to attract and keep the readers' attention with hard-hitting stories and photographs. A reporter's task is to 'news-gather'– to search out stories – and write

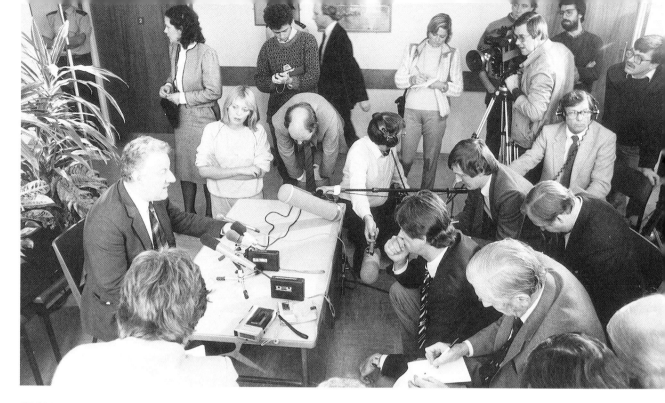

ABOVE Television, radio and print journalists at a press conference.

them up in the paper's style. A reporter can actively seek stories outside the newsroom, called off-diary stories, or write up diary stories on events of which the newspaper has been informed.

Most newsrooms have a large communal diary, which reporters share. The news editor or chief reporter marks events like council meetings, presentations and official openings in the diary in advance, and shares out the jobs as they come up. Reporters also keep in touch with local police, fire and ambulance services. On a daily paper, telephone calls may be made hourly to the emergency services; on a weekly, reporters often call in person. Other sources of news are members of the

LEFT
Other media are used to keep in touch with the latest news.

public calling or writing in with tip-offs.

Reporters have many different ways of looking for news. They keep a contacts book with the names, addresses and telephone numbers of people they know who can comment on specific topics and provide information. These contacts include police, press officers of specialist organizations, such as the RSPCA, and local authority spokespersons. Contacts are a valuable resource for a reporter, who tries to keep in touch with them on a regular, friendly basis so that if something interesting comes up, the contact will pass it on.

At the most basic level, newsgathering involves walking the streets, meeting people and staying alert for a lead which might then be researched and written up into a story. Reporters are usually trained in shorthand, typing, news writing, law and local government. This gives them the background knowledge that they need to be able to understand and interpret certain issues, as well as the skills they need to write stories up.

Reporters also have to develop skills in dealing with people. Many newspaper stories are based on arguments and disputes, and the people involved may be angry. Stories with a high news value may be very private to those

involved. As the saying goes: 'News is something that somebody doesn't want publicized. All the rest is advertising'. Much news involves human tragedies, such as car crashes, earthquakes and train disasters. Reporters have to be ready to speak to people who have lost friends or relatives to find out details of those who have died. They sometimes need to ask for a photograph of the dead person. Reporters deal with intrusion into grief in different ways; some try to get it over with quickly, while some feel that by talking with the family about their loss, they can help them to come to terms with it.

BELOW Average readership of newspapers – % of UK population, 1992.

	ANY REGIONAL	ANY REGIONAL DAILY MORNING	ANY REGIONAL DAILY EVENING	ANY LOCAL WEEKLY (FREE)	ANY LOCAL WEEKLY (PAID FOR)	ANY NATIONAL MORNING
ALL ADULTS	88.8%	11.3%	25.7%	73.2%	39.3%	63.3%
AGE						
15 - 24	85.4	9.9	27.3	66.0	38.3	64.5
25 - 34	86.3	9.9	22.9	72.0	35.2	59.0
35 - 44	89.7	11.2	23.2	76.2	40.8	62.8
45 - 54	90.9	12.5	27.5	75.1	44.3	69.2
55 - 64	90.4	13.2	28.6	73.9	41.5	67.2
65 +	90.9	11.7	25.9	76.4	37.8	60.4

ABOVE A policeman briefs reporters after a demonstration.

Once the reporter has the subject, he or she writes up the story, which must be interesting, accurate, balanced and as short as possible. The first paragraph, the 'intro', is written to grab the reader's attention. The first word of the story should be strong and descriptive: 'Homeless people are to be housed by the council' is better than 'The council are to house homeless people'. The intro should also sum up the main points of the story, preferably in under thirty words. The reporter works on the assumption that the reader is easily bored and may stop reading, therefore the main points of the story should be included in the first two paragraphs. These include the answers to the questions: who, where, what, how and why.

For accuracy, the reporter double-checks the facts and makes sure that the information in the story comes from a trustworthy source. Uncertain facts must be cross-checked with another source. The reporter must never assume. The story should be balanced; if it is about a dispute, quotations should be included from all sides, even a simple denial or 'no comment'. Direct quotations as well as reported speech from the people concerned should be used.

Reporters often work under the guidance of a chief reporter and news editor. They are part of the news-desk, which organizes news-gathering and writing. The chief reporter or news editor opens the mail and shares out routine tasks, like the coverage of courts and council meetings. The news editor suggests stories and organizes which stories are being written and when they will be finished.

BELOW Examining photographic negatives after they have been developed.

The news editor liaises with the chief sub-editor and the editor to plan what will fill each edition of the paper. Some newspapers have district offices, where reporters send in their copy via fax, computer or telephone to the newsdesk.

If stories need illustration, reporters will ask someone from the newspaper's picture department to supply a photograph. If the picture department does not have a suitable photograph, the reporter may have to get a picture agency to supply the photo. A reporter may ask one of the paper's photographers to go out and take a picture. The picture is then developed in the newspaper's own darkroom by the photographer or his or her assistant. The paper's staff photographers work under a chief photographer or picture editor who organizes their diary and liaises with the news desk.

RIGHT Photographers brave the elements at a society wedding.

The story and pictures then go into the production process. Any that are not considered good enough or cannot be checked and confirmed are 'killed' or 'spiked' – discarded. The chief sub-editor, news editor and editor decide where a story will go in the paper. According to how newsworthy it is, it could be either

a front page lead, or splash; a page lead – the largest story on an inside page; a down-page lead; a filler; a picture caption or a 'nib'. Nib stands for 'news in brief' and includes all sorts of one- or two-paragraph stories.

BELOW
A picture editor at work on screen.

The chief sub-editor then begins the process of editing the copy until it fits on the page. Often long stories end up as nibs, and most stories are shortened, simplified and checked by the sub-editors, under the guidance of the chief sub-editor. Once the advertising department informs the editorial department which spaces have been sold for adverts, the layout sub-editors design the pages, in the newspaper's style. Papers have their own rules about design, but most follow a general rule of using different typefaces for text and

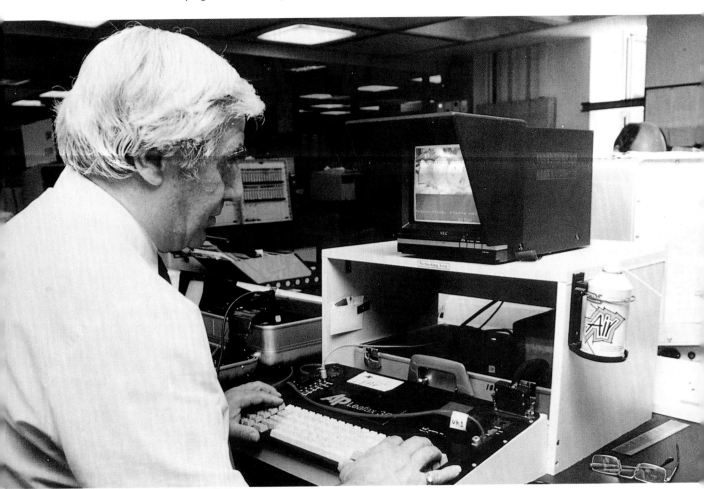

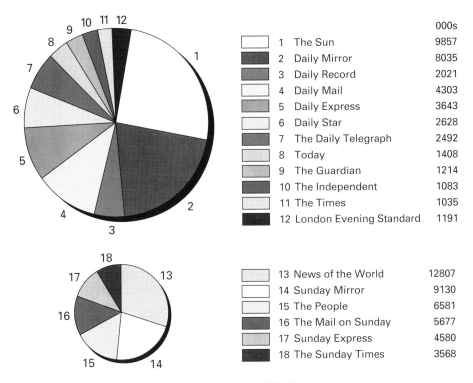

		000s
1	The Sun	9857
2	Daily Mirror	8035
3	Daily Record	2021
4	Daily Mail	4303
5	Daily Express	3643
6	Daily Star	2628
7	The Daily Telegraph	2492
8	Today	1408
9	The Guardian	1214
10	The Independent	1083
11	The Times	1035
12	London Evening Standard	1191

13	News of the World	12807
14	Sunday Mirror	9130
15	The People	6581
16	The Mail on Sunday	5677
17	Sunday Express	4580
18	The Sunday Times	3568

ABOVE Readership of leading newspapers – UK, 1991.

headlines, in different sizes and in **bold** (heavy) or roman (normal) print.

Pages are often designed around pictures. The lead picture and story are placed in position and then the rest of the page is filled up with smaller filler stories. The design is simple and straightforward so that it is clear where each story begins and ends. Sometimes layout sub-editors leave space for the headline but do not write it; this is left to the 'down-table' sub-editors, whose job it is to read and cut the story to the right length and write a headline which fits the gap exactly.

Activities

• Produce a newspaper. Make your classroom into a newsroom by dividing the class into reporters and sub-editors. Appoint a news editor, chief sub-editor and editor.

• Each reporter should write a short but interesting story, with an eye-catching introduction. Pay special attention to accuracy and use reported and direct speech. Pass the stories on to the news editor. Together, the editor and news editor should decide where the stories will go in the paper. Sub-editors should then check, correct and cut the stories and write the headlines.

• Make your own 'galley sheets' with a grid showing the overall size of the page and the way it is divided into columns. Paste up the articles, headlines and any illustrations on the pages.

More than
the news

It takes hours or even days to write, edit, design, typeset and print a newspaper for public distribution. Yet news can be broadcast on the radio almost as it happens. Television can also transmit details of events within minutes, cutting across regular programmes with newsflashes in a way that the print media cannot.

Since the spread of the electronic media, owners and editors of newspapers have realized that readers who want the latest news are more likely to turn on the TV or radio than buy a paper, and newspaper sales have fallen. But print media have an advantage over electronic news in that they are portable and the reader can look at a paper wherever and whenever he or she wants to. The newspaper has its own special place in people's lives; it is often read at meal and break times, or during travel to and from work.

BELOW
Attention-grabbing billboards aim to attract readers.

**Thursday
18 March 1993**

Jobs
start on
page 23

Sixties special   2/7

Richard Neville: Are the nineties all my fault?
Beryl Bainbridge: Where we went wrong; **George Melly**
on some great parties; **Adam Sweeting** feels mellow yellow;
Michael Billington relives a golden age; **Peter Black** on the
telly decade; **Deyan Sudjic** recalls an era of architectural promise

Also inside

Screen 8/10: Derek Malcolm joins the Teamsters; Terry Eagleton enters
the mind of Wittgenstein; **Europe 12/13:** How do you say Finnegans Wake
in Spanish? **Children's Books 14:** Six of the best for the Guardian prize;
Style 16/17: Brits storm the Bastille; **Science 18/19:** A mean time in Greenwich;
Computer 21/22: All in the mind; **Television 32; Weather 30; Radio 31**

2

*The***Guardian**

ILLUSTRATION BY PETER CLARKE (WITH APOLOGIES TO ANDY WARHOL)

**the
sixties**

the
morning
after

ABOVE The features section may include different articles about one subject.

Newspapers are also unique in that they are often shared and discussed within a group in a way that other media are not. Instead of trying to compete with other media for speed, the newspaper industry aims to attract readers with various features and services. In-depth features, investigations, sports coverage, women's pages, film and theatre reviews, advice columns, crosswords, horoscopes and cartoons are some of the non-news items included to cater for different interests. Most people have their own favourite sections which they turn to first when they open their newspaper.

Naomi tumble

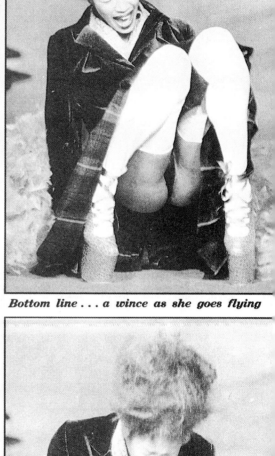

Bottom line . . . a wince as she goes flying

Kilt tilt . . . model Naomi stumbles in her eight-inch platform shoes

Platform star is all down at heel!

SUPERMODEL Naomi Campbell did a superwobble on her latest trip down the catwalk.

The £10,000-a-day British star went all weak at the knees in her eight-inch platform shoes.

She wore white leggings and a tartan kilt — just right for her own version of the Highland Fling.

Naomi twisted on the high rise stacks, crashed flat on her backside and cried out in pain.

Then Naomi, 22, collapsed again into tears of laughter. Her giggles brought the house down as everyone at Vivienne Westwood's Paris show saw the funny side.

An onlooker said: "Naomi fell into a real heap. The audience was in no doubt about the colour of her knickers."

After the show her friend Yasmine Eslami revealed: "Naomi thought it was hilarious. Fortunately she didn't hurt herself."

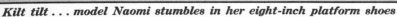

It's a scream . . in pain after fall Pictures: KEN TOWNE

Some writers in the features department come up with articles that either provide background information or else a lighter, more entertaining angle on the news. While news stories present the facts, news features aim to make readers understand their significance. For example, a paper might carry a front page story about the latest developments in a prison riot that has gone on for a few days. This might be followed a few pages later with an article by a features writer looking at rising crime and overcrowding in prisons. The features department concentrates on summing up after an event or providing an advance guide. For example, before the Olympics many newspapers publish large pull-out sections with details of all the forthcoming events and competitors; and after a general election, commentaries and a full round-up of results may be printed.

LEFT
Even a minor mishap by a famous personality makes big news.

Other features writers become experts on certain topics, and sometimes personalities in their own right. Political columnists, women's page editors and showbusiness writers often have 'picture bylines' – a picture of themselves alongside their name. Sometimes politicians, sports stars or people with expertise on a particular subject may be contracted to write articles.

Gossip columns concentrate exclusively on famous personalities, and are often illustrated by unposed photographs, taken by the 'paparazzi' – photographers who specialize in snatching

BELOW Regional readership of leading UK newspapers – 1991.

	TOTAL		LONDON & SOUTH EAST		SOUTH WEST & WALES		MIDLANDS		NORTH WEST		NORTH EAST & NORTH		SCOTLAND	
	000	%	000	%	000	%	000	%	000	%	000	%	000	%
THE SUN	9857	22	3785	24	1304	21	1817	25	753	14	1381	21	816	20
DAILY MIRROR & RECORD	10001	22	2815	18	1143	19	1341	18	1259	24	1429	22	2015	49
DAILY MAIL	4303	10	2055	13	671	11	630	9	447	9	432	7	66	2
DAILY EXPRESS	3643	8	1403	9	474	8	439	6	542	10	491	8	294	7
THE DAILY TELEGRAPH	2492	6	1286	8	355	6	288	4	286	5	217	3	59	1
TODAY	1408	3	555	4	214	3	235	3	177	3	185	3	42	1
THE GUARDIAN	1214	3	604	4	133	2	149	2	165	3	127	2	35	1
THE INDEPENDENT	1083	2	611	4	128	2	108	1	94	2	84	1	57	1
THE TIMES	1035	2	668	4	115	2	100	1	60	1	56	1	37	1

shots of famous people. In interviews, feature writers present a 'word portrait' of the interviewee, not only finding out and recording the basic facts, but also including personal details. The writer aims to make the readers feel as if they have met the person interviewed.

Many readers buy a newspaper for the information contained on the leisure pages. Television and radio programmes and times are listed as well as details of cinemas and theatres. Reviews and previews provide information about the quality of what is on offer.

Newspapers are divided up into sections for different parts of the readership. The women's page, although often read by men, contains articles which are thought to be of particular interest to women. Many readers consider the sports coverage to be the most important part of their paper, and it is usually placed where it is easy to find: at the back of the paper with its own 'front page' on the back page. The sports pages include full results, as well as features, future fixtures and tips.

Newspapers also aim to provide a service for their readers, who can write in for advice on different problems: personal on the Agony Aunt's page, medical and financial. The letters page gives readers a chance to air their grievances and opinions. Other popular sections of the newspaper, which are often syndicated (meaning that they are bought in from outside services), are cartoons, crosswords, puzzles and horoscopes.

LEFT Agony Aunt Marjorie Proops.

Advertisements are an important part of newspapers. Local papers depend on them for finance, although national newspapers make most of their income from newspaper sales.

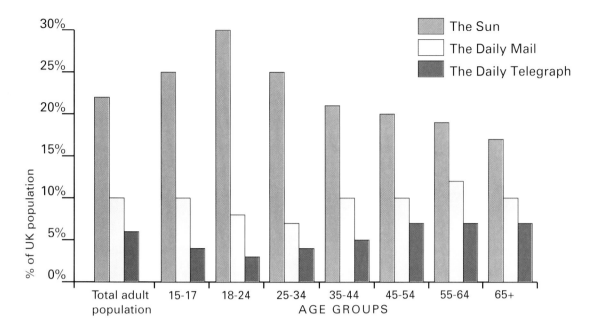

ABOVE Readership levels of three UK national newspapers among different age groups, 1991.

Advertising can be divided into two types. Display ads are usually large and include artwork, while classified ads are made up of standard-sized type and are arranged according to subject. The classified section includes notices of births, marriages and deaths; items wanted; animals, property and cars for sale and homes for rent.

Competitions and games also help boost readership, and most newspapers have a department which organizes promotions. In games like bingo, readers are given their own personal game cards, and numbers are printed in the newspaper. There are often large cash prizes. This helps to attract and maintain high circulations, as readers need to buy the paper every day to check their numbers. Rival newspapers sometimes wage fierce circulation wars against each other using promotional competitions with ever-increasing prizes.

Activities

• Conduct a survey among your parents, relatives and friends to find out why they read newspapers. You could ask them what their favourite and least-liked parts of a newspaper are; what they read first; what they never read; which newspapers they buy and where they read their newspaper.

• Write up your findings as if they were a feature in a newspaper, and illustrate them with graphs and charts.

The freedom
of the press

News stories are often based round an event that somebody, somewhere had been hoping to keep secret. Exposés – stories which uncover hidden facts – are a powerful way to attract readers. Although television and radio produce investigative programmes, it is the newspaper press which has claimed for itself the role of exposing the wrongdoings of personalities, politicians and companies.

The people involved want to keep the stories secret for different reasons. It could be because they have broken the law, or because they stand to lose out politically or financially if public opinion turns against them; for example, a politician in a sex scandal or a company selling faulty goods. Journalists cannot afford to be intimidated by the power and reputation of the people involved; the bigger the name, the bigger the scandal. The role of 'snoop' means that journalists are often deservedly unpopular. They often have to intrude into the most private parts of their subjects' lives. Their techniques include: 'doorstepping' – waiting outside the subject's home for twenty-four hours a day, telephone tapping, and paying for information from friends or neighbours.

However, there are laws that exist in most countries to safeguard a citizen's right to keep his or her affairs private. In Britain, the law of defamation aims to protect the personal and professional reputation of the individual. When a defamatory statement is printed or broadcast it is libel; when spoken it is slander. An individual who feels he or she has been libelled can take action through the courts. The person can attempt to claim compensation for damages in the same way as someone who has been physically damaged. He or she must prove that the statement would be considered defamatory by average members of society.

RIGHT Security at Wapping, the News International headquarters in England. Controlled by Rupert Murdoch, News International newspapers include The *Sun* and *The Times*.

To be defamatory, the statement must have caused the individual to be avoided, ridiculed or hated, either in his or her job, or by society in general. Because public opinion changes, what is considered to be defamatory also changes; in Britain during the First World War, to write that a person was German was considered to be libellous.

British law also protects people who are involved in court cases, who are assumed to be innocent until proven guilty. There are strict rules that govern what newspapers can print before, during and after trials. These aim to balance the right of the public to information and the individual's right to a fair trial. This is to prevent 'trial by media', when the jury could be influenced by advance discussion in newspapers or television reports of the trial. Reporters are allowed into court, but their accounts of what happens must be fair and accurate, and published as close to the time of the hearing as possible. They must not break any legal restrictions laid down by the judge. In some cases, judges will make special rulings to protect children involved, such as preventing journalists from reporting their names.

ABOVE Newspapers sometimes go a bit too far in their attempts to provoke political debate. This advert had to be withdrawn after complaints from members of the public.

Photographers are not allowed to take photographs in court, although they do sometimes snatch pictures of subjects entering or leaving the building. Newspapers are not allowed to use the photos if the trial hinges on identity. As well as protecting individuals, British law has established the right of a newspaper to publish news that is in the public interest, so long as articles are fair and factual. Anything said in court, Parliament or a public meeting is covered by 'privilege', which allows the paper to report it.

The freedom of the press to publish is important in a free society. The growth of the popular newspaper press coin-cided with the rise of democracy – the freedom of people to choose who governs them. Newspapers were seen as a way of educating the general public so that they could make well-informed and responsible decisions when it came to voting.

Newspapers were regarded as an essential part of a civilized society. They were among the first organizations to be set up by the British in countries which they had colonized. In New Zealand, a newspaper was founded soon after the first immigrant ships began to arrive in the 1840s. Newspapers were also seen as defenders of the public interest; one, The *Poor Man's*

Guardian, had 'Knowledge is Power' printed on every issue. Today, a fair and independent newspaper press is thought to be vital for investigating and exposing corruption and wrongdoing which would otherwise remain hidden from the public. In most countries, newspapers have to stay within certain rules controlling what they publish. This is especially true in times of war and unrest, when some stories could endanger national security.

The newspaper industry has traditionally fought hard to protect its right to free speech and freedom of information.

Editors have argued that, in a democracy, they should be allowed to decide what is published without interference from the government. However, this 'self-regulation' often breaks down when newspapers are competing for readers. Editors often cannot resist the temptation to publish a scoop, even if it breaks their own rules about privacy.

Although the press can be a powerful watchdog in a free society, it can also be used to promote and uphold governments and rulers who take away peoples' freedoms. Politicians have long understood

BELOW
In Saudi Arabia, photos of kissing couples are censored – even if they are royal!

Daily Telegraph

),778.   THURSDAY, JULY 31, 1986   Printed in LONDON and MANCHESTER   25p

Join the
ASTHMA
SOCIETY
For advise on asthma and how to cope. You will receive Asthma News and other helpful information.
Send stamp for information to Hugh Faulkner, ASTHMA SOCIETY, 300 Upper Street, London N1 2XX

Miss Susannah Lamplugh—still missing after three days.

Kilroy-Silk quits for BBC

By George Jones
Political Correspondent

LABOUR'S attempts to present a new moderate image suffered a blow last night when Mr Robert Kilroy-Silk announced he was resigning as an MP because he had been "driven out of politics by the Militant Tendency."

Mr Kilroy-Silk, 44, is quitting for a career in television as chairman of a new "popular discussion programme" on the BBC.

He plans to resign his safe Labour seat of Knowsley North, merseyside, in the autumn, forcing a by-election. At the General Election he had a majority of 17,191 over the Conservatives

His decision took Labour's leadership by surprise last night and clearly angered a number of fellow MPs. But over the past three years he has been involved in a debilitating struggle with extreme Left-wingers in his constituency.

Generally acknowledged to be one of the brighter

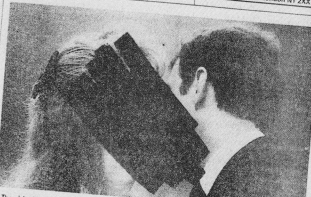

The blacked-out kiss as seen by readers of The Daily Telegraph special Royal Wedding supplement in Saudi Arabia.

Missing girl 'lying bound' say parents

By IAN HENRY, Crime C

Home loan debt warning

By George Jones

Saudi censors blot out Royal kiss

By KENNETH CLARKE and NIGEL DUDLEY

that what people think can be controlled and influenced by the press. All papers have their own viewpoint on the world, or ideology. In a free society, with a free press, there usually exists a range of papers to present different points of view. In countries where no political parties are allowed to oppose the government, newspapers are controlled by the government and are used to support its ideas.

Sometimes newspapers have to go 'underground' to survive, for example, the papers which played a part in helping countries that were once ruled by Britain in their struggle for independence. When India was ruled by the British in the seventeenth and eighteenth centuries, there were restrictions on newspapers printed in local languages. This was because they addressed the people directly and aimed to organize opposition. These papers became important tools in supporting the movement towards home rule. In the Soviet Union, the newspaper of the Communist Party, *Pravda* ('Truth'), dominated. A thriving underground press of *samizdat* (self-publishing) newspapers put forward opposing political views and ideas.

With the collapse of the communist government, *Pravda* managed to survive only by changing its editorial position – the point of view it took on certain subjects.

Newspapers often try to keep obviously biased articles to one section of the paper; for example, unsigned editorial columns about current events. During elections, papers may come down in favour of one political party, but usually they present articles as objective – factual and without bias.

Sometimes the angle taken on a story is biased. When the British national daily tabloid The *Sun* covered a tragedy at a football match where more than 100 fans died, it concentrated on reporting the bad behaviour of supporters. This was not one of the main reasons why the disaster occurred. In this case, the bias had gone too far and public outrage and a drop in sales led to an apology from the paper.

When journalists write a story, they have to write from a single point of view – their own. Usually, the copy is not obviously biased towards what the journalist thinks about the subject. However, the journalist has to make choices about what to leave out of the article. This means that one person's point of view might be given in the piece, while another point of view is ignored. For example, a politician rather than a famine victim might be asked to comment about a famine. So the article may tend to emphasize the problems of giving aid to starving peoples, rather than the tragedy of famine.

Editors argue that this 'hidden bias' already exists in society and that the contents of a newspaper merely reflect it. How far newspapers control public opinion is a matter of debate. Many would argue that with their semi-nude models, aggressively patriotic campaigns and political bias presented as a general viewpoint, some newspapers reinforce harmful stereotypes. On the other hand, research has shown that people do not necessarily agree with views expressed in newspapers that they regularly buy. But people read newspapers not only for information on the latest events, but also to gain a sense of what is important and a 'way of seeing' society.

Today, most newspapers are run as businesses, to make money. But the newspaper industry's role extends beyond profit. Newspapers entertain, educate and reflect the society they serve, and provide a lasting record of events for future generations.

Activities
Using a tabloid, a broadsheet and a local newspaper, make a list of the subjects covered in all the articles in one edition. Divide the list into categories such as human interest, court cases, political news and business news. Find examples of: political bias; sexual stereotypes; racial stereotypes; invasions of privacy. Compare the different types of bias in different newspapers.

glossary

Banner headline
A large, bold, eye-catching headline.

Bias
Prejudice, or leaning towards a particular way of thinking.

Byline
The name of the journalist, printed at the top of a story or feature.

Caption
Information printed with and about a photograph.

Circulation
The number of readers of a newspaper.

Columnist
A journalist or celebrity who writes a newspaper feature (column) in which they express their own opinions.

Contempt of court
To go against the authority of a lawcourt.

Copy
Written material for inclusion in a newspaper.

Defamation
To say or write something that harms the reputation of somebody or something.

Edit
To make a piece of writing ready to be published in a newspaper, book or magazine by checking facts, correcting spelling or grammatical mistakes and improving the clarity of the writing.

Edition
A set of identical newspapers published at the same time.

Editorial
Stories, features and photographs produced under the direction of the newspaper's editor.

Filler
A small story often used to fill up the bottom of the page.

Headline
The title of a story, usually appearing in bold print above the copy.

Media
The press, including television, radio and newspapers.

Newsprint
Lightweight, inexpensive paper used for printing newspapers.

Newsroom

The department where editorial staff, including reporters and sub-editors, work.

Off-the-record

A description applied to information given to a journalist which is not for direct publication or must not be attributed to the source.

Press release

Information given to the press by an organization or individual in the form of an official letter or announcement. Press releases are sent to the press when an organization wants journalists to attend an important event, or when people wish to make their views on a news story known to the public.

Review

An article outlining and judging the merits of a play, film or book, or of a commercial product such as a newly manufactured car.

Scoop

An item of major news interest which a newspaper is the first to publish.

Sensational

Aimed at producing a startling impression.

Serial

A story published in instalments.

Splash

A newspaper term for a front-page lead story.

Stereotype

A fixed, often negative, image of a person or group of people.

Type

Printed letters produced by various methods. Originally, type was blocks of metal or wood each with a raised letter or character on one end; it now more often takes the form of computer-printed lettering and other symbols.

Typeface

The style and design of letters of type. The typeface used in this book is called Univers. *The Times* uses Times, The *Daily Mail* uses **Ionic** and The *Independent* uses Plantin.

Typeset

To make written copy into type ready for printing.

further reading

F.W. Hodgson, *Modern Newspaper Practice* (Heinemann, 1984)

Alan J. Lee, *The Origins of the Popular Press 1855-1914* (Croom Helm Roman and Littlefield, 1980)

Brenda Mann, *Newspapers* (Wayland, 1987)

The Newspaper Society, *The Making of a Newspaper* (1993)

Anthony Smith, *The Newspaper; An International History* (Thames and Hudson, 1983)

Iris Webb, *Bias in the Media* and *Stereotyping in the Media* (Wayland, 1993)

further information and notes for teachers

Newspapers in Education, run by the Newspaper Society, has an educational resources catalogue which includes many publications about, and featuring the work of, newspapers. It is available from The Newspaper Society, Bloomsbury House, 74-77 Great Russell Street, London WC1B 3DA, England

Other useful addresses include:

The American Newspaper Publishers
  Association
The Newspaper Center
Box 17407
Dallas Airport
Washington DC
20041
USA

The Canadian Daily Newspapers
  Association
890 Yonge Street
STE 1100
Toronto
ON M4W 3PA
Canada

The Newspaper Publishers Association Ltd.
34 Southwark Bridge Road
London SE1 9EU
England

The Newspaper Publishers Association
  of New Zealand
Newspaper House
93 Boulcutt Street
PO Box 1066
Wellington 1
New Zealand

index numbers in **bold** refer to captions

advertising **5**, 6,19, **20**, 30, 36, 37, **40**
Agony Aunts 36
Australia **9**

Beaverbrook, Lord 8
bias 21,43,44
books 4
broadsheets 9,23,44

circulation 9,37
competitions 37
computers 15,16,28
content of newspapers 32
copy 8,15,16,28,30,44

design 9,16,21,30,31

editors 8,20,21,28,31,32
electric telegraphs 6
Europe 4,5

features **33**, 35
filler stories 30,31
format of newspapers 21,32-8
freedom of the press 38-44
front pages 19,21,30,35

gossip columns 21,35

headlines 4,21,31
Hearst, William Randolph 8
human interest stories 20,44

interviewing 26,36
investigative journalism 23,38,41

journalism 18-23,24-6
journalists 8, 15, 16, 18, 20, 23, 24, 25, 26, 27, 28, 35, 38, 44

laws and restrictions 38-44
    defamation laws 23, 38, 39
lead stories 30,31
local papers 8,9,36

middle market papers 21
Murdoch, Rupert 8,**9**

national papers 9,36
New Journalism 20
news agencies 6
news-gathering 18-23, 24, 25,26,28,38
    snoop reporting 38
newsheets 4
newspapers
    history and development of 4-10, 19, 20,21,40,43
    ownership of 8,32
    role of newspapers in society 38-44
newsrooms **15**,25
newsroom diaries 25,28
news value 18,19
New Zealand 40
Northcliffe, Lord 8

paper production 6
photographers **18**,24,28,40
    paparazzi 35
photographs 16,24,26,28,35,40,**41**
Press Association 8
press barons 8
press releases 18
printing 6,8,9,10-17,19,24
printing presses 4,10,**11**
production 10-16,24-31
Pulitzer, Joseph 20

Reuters 6
review articles 33,36
Rothermere, Lord 8

sensationalism in news stories 19,20
sources of news 23, 25, 27
sports articles 20, 33, 35, 36
sub-editors 15, 16, 28, 30, 31

tabloids 9,21,23,44
television 8,18,24,32,38
typefaces 16,31
typesetters **11**,15,16

USA 8,13,15,20,**43**

web-offset press 13
women's pages 33,35,36
writing news stories 18, 19, 20, 21, 23, 25, 26, 27, 28, 44